RICE®

www.mascotbooks.com

Count On™ Rice®: Fun Facts from 1 to 12

For more information, please contact:
Mascot Books
560 Herndon Parkway #120
Herndon, VA 20170
info@mascotbooks.com

CPSIA Code: PRT0716A
ISBN-13: 978-1-63177-532-1

Printed in the United States

COUNT ON ™
RICE ®

Fun Facts from 1 to 12

by Robin A. Ward, Ph.D.

Rice has **one** mascot.
His name is Sammy the Owl.

Our school's **two** colors are blue and gray.
At games, our fans howl!

3

Three stories comprise Duncan Hall,
its interior as colorful as can be.

4

Rice's Academic Quadrangle has **four** sides.
Count them and you'll see!

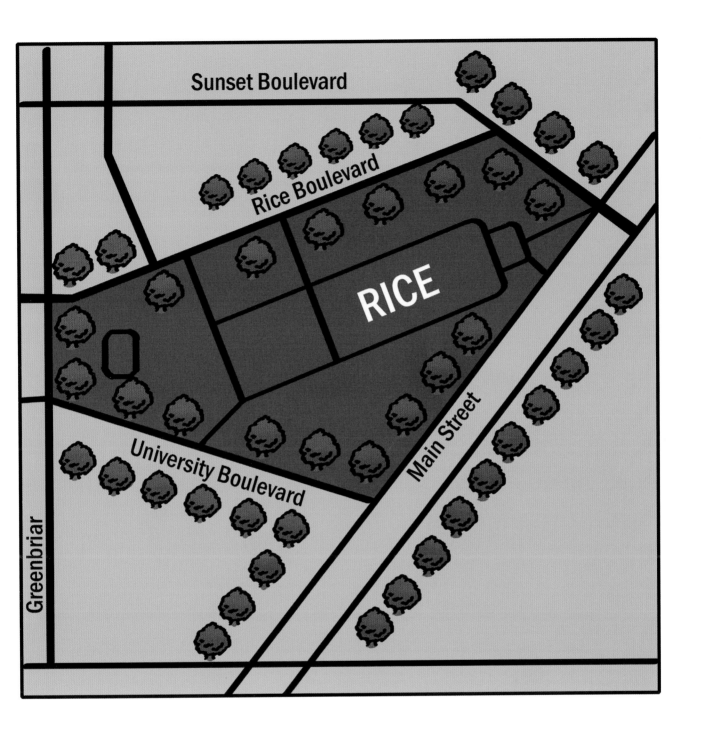

Five streets shape Rice's campus,
all lined with trees.

Six is the number of schools
that offer undergraduate degrees.

Seven was the year in 1900 when Edgar Odell Lovett was named Rice's first president.

Eight Rice Owls were selected in the 2012 MLB draft. On the field, they weren't hesitant!

Nine Rice faculty are members
of the prestigious National Academy of Sciences,
and we know there will be more.

10

Ten was the number of faculty hired when Rice first opened its doors.

Eleven is the number of Residential Colleges in which undergraduates dwell.

Twelve was the year in 1900 when
Rice Institute's first classes were held.

I wish we could keep counting!

But instead, I'll offer some advice.

If you ever want to count again,

why not count on **Rice?**

A Note to Parents

Notice that the *even* numbers in this book appear in gray and the *odd* numbers in blue.

Guide your reader to discover that even numbers can be grouped into pairs, indicated by the owls placed vertically two-by-two on each left-hand page. You cannot create pairs with an odd number of objects, as you will always have one odd man (I mean, owl) out!

On each left-hand page, notice that the number of images around each numeral represents that number as well.

Why count to 12 instead of stopping at 10? Notice that the illustrations capture the changing of the seasons during the 12 months. And, Rice just celebrated its centennial birthday in 2012!

Enjoy coloring the two coloring pages that follow.

Go Owls!

Sammy the Owl loves the Rice Owls!

About the Author

Robin is a Professor of Mathematics and the Director of Curriculum Integration for the Rice University School Mathematics Project. Her husband, Chris DelConte, is the Director of Athletics at TCU, and was Rice's AD from 2006-2009. They have two daughters, Sienna and Sophia.

Robin's career includes working as an aerospace engineer and a NASA educational consultant, and her extensive research has been published nationally and internationally. She is the author of five teacher resource books on using the visual arts and children's literature in the K-8 mathematics classroom. She is regularly heard encouraging teachers and students to put on their *math goggles*® as a way to see math in art and in their world.

Robin is the author of *Count on TCU: Fun Facts from 1 to 12.*

Robin's ultimate personal goal is for all students to fall in love with mathematics.

So, let's begin by counting...*Count on Rice!*

What colors would you want inside of Duncan Hall?

Use your imagination!